Family Walks in the New Forest

Nigel Vile

HIGH INTEREST · LOW MILEAGE

Scarthin Books of Cromford
Derbyshire
1993

Family Walks in the New Forest

General Editor: Norman Taylor

The Countryside Code

Respect the life and work of the countryside
Guard against the risk of fire
Fasten all gates
Keep dogs under close control
Keep to the public paths across farmland
Use gates or stiles to cross fences, hedges and walls
Leave livestock, crops and machinery alone
Take all your litter home
Help to keep all water clean
Protect wildlife, plants and trees
Take care on country roads
Make no unnecessary noise

Walking the routes in this book

All the routes in this book have been walked, in most cases, several times prior to publication and we have taken great care to ensure that they are on rights of way. However, changes occur all the time in the landscape; should you meet any obstructions, please let us know. Serious obstructions can be brought to the attention of the local branch of the Ramblers Association and the Rights of Way section of the County Council.

Published 1993 by Scarthin Books of Cromford, Derbyshire

Printed in Great Britain at The Alden Press, Oxford

ISBN 0907758 606

Cover illustration by Andrew Ravenwood

Great Linford Inclosure – route 4.

Acknowledgements

Many thanks to my wife Gill for drawing the maps, and to my sister-in-law Trisha for the sketches that accompany some of the walks. My thanks also go to my own children – Laura, Katie and James – for being patient guinea-pigs!

About the author

Nigel Vile currently teaches at King Edward's School in Bath. He was born in Bristol more years ago than he cares to remember, and currently lives in the Wiltshire town of Bradford-on-Avon. As well as this book of rambles, he is also the author of companion volumes that cover Bath and Bristol, Wiltshire and Mendip, Sedgemoor and Avalon. He is also a regular contributor to the *Down Your Way* section of *Country Walking* magazine.

Contents

Map of the area

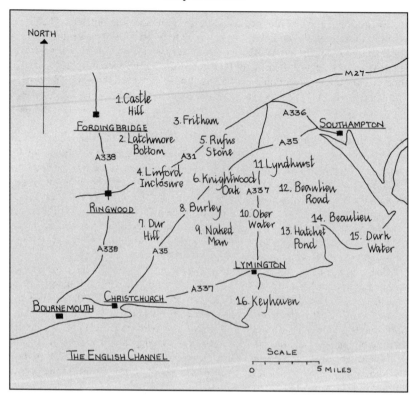

NORTH

M27

1. Castle Hill

FORDINGBRIDGE

3. Fritham

A336

SOUTHAMPTON

2. Latchmore Bottom

5. Rufus Stone

A35

A338

A31

4. Limford Inclosure

11. Lyndhurst

6. Knightwood Oak A337

12. Beaulieu Road

RINGWOOD

8. Burley

10. Ober Water

14. Beaulieu

7. Dur Hill

9. Naked Man

13. Hatchet Pond

15. Dark Water

A338

A35

LYMINGTON

A337

CHRISTCHURCH

16. Keyhaven

BOURNEMOUTH

THE ENGLISH CHANNEL

SCALE

0   5 MILES

Preface

I write about and explore the New Forest very much as an outsider. The Forest is one of those special places that I have grown to treasure as a visitor, both on day trips and camping holidays. Viewed from across the border in Wiltshire, the residents of this delightful corner of Hampshire are a privileged people indeed! The thoughts and comments of outsiders should not be dismissed, however. We are less parochial in our outlook, less xenophobic about our favourite patch of the woods. We can write with an overall picture of the area, uncoloured by local passion or preserve.

The New Forest is indeed a special place. It is now over 900 years since William the Conqueror enacted his Forest Laws, designed to preserve the beasts of the chase. To this day, the Forest is the largest area of unenclosed land in southern England, a walker's paradise with virtually free-access rights to every nook and cranny of its 92,000 acres. The guidebooks talk of "stepping back in time" when visiting the Forest, of an area where traditions have remained virtually unchanged since medieval times. This is the beauty of the area. The commoners and verderers, the agisters and the keepers, have combined to ensure that the Forest is a legacy to be preserved for all time as a prime aspect of the nation's heritage.

There is tremendous pressure on the New Forest from tourism. London lies within a couple of hours drive, meaning that literally millions of visitors view the area as being in their backyard. Nothing is more depressing than the sight of car-parks full of visitors, afraid to venture more than a few feet from their vehicle. I hope that this book will go some way towards curing this malaise! Once beyond the secure confines of the Forestry Commission's parking lots, it is possible to find solitude and beauty, as well as features of much fascination and interest. With these few thoughts in mind, I commend this collection of walks to you as the perfect antidote to the pressures of modern living!

Symbols used on the route maps

	roads		settlement
	path or track		river or stream
+	church	· 121'	spot heights
P	parking space	△ 120'	trig points
PH ·	public house	→	direction indicator
	deciduous woodland		coniferous woodland
	mixed woodland	A35 → LYNDHURST	title and destination of selected road
6	number corresponding with directions		pond or lake
START	start of walk		selected building

8

Godshill Inclosure and Castle Hill

Outline
Godshill Wood car-park – Densome Corner – Godshill Inclosure – Castle Hill – Godshill Wood – Godshill Inclosure – Car-park.

Summary
The north-western boundary of the New Forest is marked by a plateau of high ground overlooking the Hampshire Avon and the more distant Cranborne Chase. The grassy ditches and banks that line the hilltop are believed to be the only remaining Norman fortifications within the Forest. Also included in this 3-mile circuit is the opportunity to explore the adjoining Godshill Inclosure, an area of mixed woodland containing oak, sweet chestnut, rowan and pines.

Attractions
Nature provides a rich harvest of edible fruits, nuts and berries. During the early stages of this walk, alongside and through Godshill Inclosure, a veritable natural feast could be gathered. Crab apples, blackberries, bilberries, sweet chestnuts and beech nuts represent just some of nature's great bounty that can be unearthed on this ramble. The potential food supply from our hedgerows and woodlands is vast, and has been well-documented in books such as *Pick, Cook and Brew* by Suzanne Beedell (Mayflower Books). Whilst bramble jelly and elderberry wine might grace any table-top, I am less certain about the potential of nettle fritters or dandelion puree! Personally, I would recommend a stroll through Godshill Inclosure in the autumn months, when the sweet chestnuts are in season. There is little in nature's harvest to rival the roast chestnut.

The River Avon is one of the great rivers of southern Britain. From its source in the Vale of Pewsey, it dissects the chalk country of Salisbury Plain before flowing through the sands and clays of the Hampshire Basin. It finally joins the River Stour at the head of Christchurch Harbour before entering the English Channel. English Nature describe the Avon as showing "a greater range of habitat diversity and a more diverse flora and fauna than any other chalk river in Britain." Ragged robin and marsh marigold, Bewick's swans and grey herons, great crested grebe and salmon . . . the list of species is virtually endless. Unfortunately, the nearest this walk comes to the Avon is a rather fine view of the river from Castle Hill. The good news, however, is the fact that Hampshire County Council have recently waymarked the Avon Valley Path between Salisbury Cathedral and Christchurch Priory – excellent free leaflets can be obtained from local tourist information centres.

Castle Hill runs for almost 1 mile between the villages of Godshill and Woodgreen, in the extreme north-western corner of the New Forest. The hill derives its name from a series of ancient earthworks, thought by experts to be the only remaining Norman fortifications in the Forest. Their location is quite superb – high

Continued on page 12

Route 1

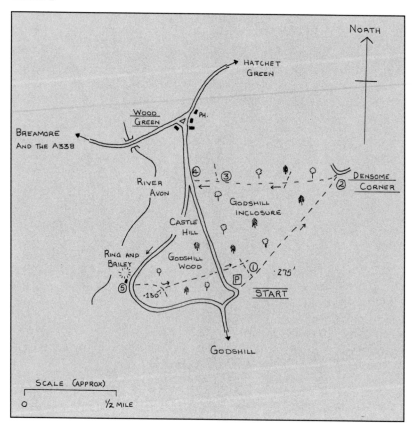

NORTH

HATCHET GREEN

WOOD GREEN

PH.

BREAMORE AND THE A338

RIVER AVON

④ ③

② DENSOME CORNER

GODSHILL INCLOSURE

CASTLE HILL

RING AND BAILEY

GODSHILL WOOD

⑤ ·150'

① ·275'

P

START

GODSHILL

SCALE (APPROX)

0   ½ MILE

10

Route 1

Godshill Inclosure and Castle Hill   3 miles

Start

Leave the A338 at Breamore, and follow the unclassified road signposted to Wood Green. Turn right in this village to follow the Godshill turning and, in 1 mile, park on the left-hand side in the Godshill Wood car-park. GR 177161.

1. Walk to the end of the car-park and follow the path alongside Godshill Inclosure for ¾ mile until you reach Densome Corner and the Wood Green to Hatchet Green road. On your left at this point, there is a handgate leading into the inclosure.

2. Enter the inclosure and follow the woodland path for ¼ mile to a cross-track. Follow the path opposite for almost ½ mile, ignoring several side turns and cross-tracks.

3. Where this gravelled path forks to the right by a group of oak trees, bear left onto a smaller path that soon joins the Godshill to Wood Green road.

4. Turn right and, almost immediately, left onto the lane signposted 'Castle Hill'. Follow this lane across Castle Hill for over ½ mile, pausing at the viewpoints to enjoy glimpses of the River Avon, until you reach a cottage on the right-hand side named 'Armsley'.
   NB. To reach the hillfort, turn right onto a path marked by some wooden posts just before the cottage. At the top of a rise, bear right past a second cottage to reach the fortifications. Retrace your steps to the road.

5. Opposite 'Armsley', a gate leads into Godshill Wood. 300 yards into the woodland, bear left at a fork and continue on through the trees to the Wood Green road. Cross the road, and enter Godshill Inclosure. In another 300 yards, turn right at a cross-track and follow one final woodland path back to the car-park.

Public Transport

Maybury Coaches operate a Salisbury to Wood Green and Fordingbridge service that passes the start of the walk.

on the hilltop with steep slopes tumbling down to the banks of the Avon. Defensively, it would be difficult to find a more secure site. The 'Ring and Bailey' site lies at the southern end of Castle Hill, and is now well-hidden by surrounding woodland. Fortunately, two fine viewpoints have been opened up to the north of the castle site, bringing expansive views across the Avon Valley.

Refreshments
Alongside the car-park, there is an excellent area of open grassland where visitors can enjoy a picnic. In Wood Green, just 1 mile from the car-park, refreshments can be obtained in the Horse and Groom Inn.

Hampton Ridge and Latchmore Bottom

Outline
Abbots Well – Hampton Ridge – Alderhill Inclosure – Latchmore Bottom – Abbots Well.

Summary
The north-western corner of the New Forest is characterised by a series of parallel valleys separated by relatively high ridges. This excursion – surprisingly hilly for the New Forest – explores the hilltops around Hampton Ridge, before descending into Latchmore Bottom. This valley is a marvellously secluded place, watered by the Latchmore Brook, where the Forest lawns and the running stream attract large numbers of Forest ponies. An excellent walk in a corner of the Forest that lies somewhat off the beaten track.

Attractions
At the start of the walk, our steps pass two circular depressions by the side of the road, containing plentiful supplies of fresh water – the spot known as 'Abbots Well'. Despite recourse to every local guidebook that I could find, the well remains a mystery – unchronicled and unrecorded. One can but speculate! Twenty miles to the south lies the site of Christchurch Priory, built in 1094, whilst 15 miles to the north we have the important ecclesiastical centre of Salisbury. Who can say whether Abbots Well marked a spot of refreshment for some wandering cleric in centuries past? Certainly, with its fine views of Hampton Ridge it is an uplifting and inspiring place.

Despite its present-day seclusion, this area of the Forest was the site of important trade routes in centuries past. Tradesmen carrying local pottery, made from clay deposits in the north-west of the Forest, would have crossed Hampton Ridge to reach the Avon Valley and markets beyond. An archaeological dig at a Roman camp near Old Sarum, for example, unearthed a significant haul of New Forest pottery. Of lesser significance were the 'fern tracks' that ran through Latchmore Bottom. The Forest's commoners would carry cartloads of bracken through the valley to be used for a variety of traditional uses. These might include bedding for their animals or covering for their vegetable clamps.

Latchmore Bottom, with its excellent grazing and the waters of the Latchmore Brook, is a natural focus for local ponies. Ponies have wandered freely through the Forest since time immemorial. This was their habitat long before William the Conqueror made the Forest his hunting preserve. Many local experts maintain that the ponies actually hark back to the genuinely wild stock that roamed through the ancient forests of primeval Britain. Despite their unkempt appearance, however, the ponies all have their owners. These are the commoners, whose right to free-grazing dates back to the time when William prohibited the enclosure of

Continued on page 16

13

Route 2

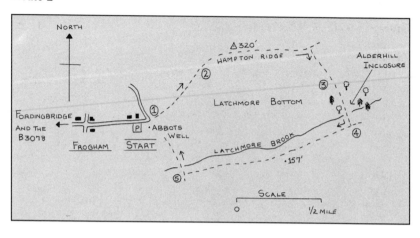

Route 2

Hampton Ridge and Latchmore Bottom   3 miles

Start
Just east of Fordingbridge, leave the B3078 Cadnam road and follow the unclassified lane signposted to Stuckton and Frogham. In Frogham, continue along this lane, now signposted to 'Abbots Well'. Just before you reach the actual well, there is a large parking area on the right-hand side. GR 177128.

1. *Return to the road from the car-park, turn right and walk the few yards down to the site of Abbots Well. Ahead is a vast area of open heathland. Follow the obvious winding path ahead that climbs up onto Hampton Ridge.*

2. *Follow the main path across the ridge, passing the trig point on your left-hand side. $\frac{1}{2}$ mile on from this trig point, the path forks. Bear right and follow the path across the hilltop then downhill towards Alderhill Inclosure.*

3. *A handgate takes you into the inclosure, where you follow the path ahead through to the far side of this mainly coniferous woodland. En route, you will have to cross a ford through Latchmore Brook.*

4. *Leave the woodland at a handgate and turn right. Follow the path ahead for over 1 mile, through Latchmore Bottom. For much of the way, the river is hidden in the trees to your right. Frequent detours to the water's edge are in order!*

5. *At the far end of Latchmore Bottom, you will reach a parking area. Turn right, cross the footbridge over Latchmore Brook (or paddle through the adjoining ford) and follow the well-defined path beyond up Windmill Hill and back to Abbots Well. Turn left at the road to retrace your steps to the car-park.*

Public Transport
Maybury Coaches operate a Salisbury to Fordingbridge service that passes through Frogham, 10 minutes walk from Abbots Well.

agricultural land – fences would have interfered with the royal deer chase! All of the Forest's ponies have their tail hair clipped in a unique way to prove their right to graze freely on the open land. This clipping is performed by a team of four agisters, who regularly patrol the Forest keeping an eye on its livestock.

Whatever else you do, do not feed the ponies. If they become dependent upon humans for their food supply, the ponies would gravitate towards the car-parks and roads with obvious consequences for their safety.

Refreshments
The banks of Latchmore Brook, with its excellent paddling potential, would make a good spot for a picnic. Just minutes from the end of the walk, you will find the Foresters Arms in Frogham.

Pony drinking in Eyeworth Pond

Fritham and Eyeworth Pond

Outline
Fritham – Eyeworth Pond – Irons Well – Howens Bushes – Fritham.

Summary
This delightful walk in the north-western corner of the Forest encapsulates all that is best about the area. A Forest village with its traditional pub, a fine pond with its feeder stream, deciduous woodland, open heath and a rich variety of wildlife. The mileage on this particular walk is minimal, and the terrain easy-going, which makes it a perfect circuit for even the smallest of toddlers.

Attractions
Fritham is one of those idyllic English villages that every expatriot Englishman must dream of. Picturesque cottages and a traditional pub overlooking the village green . . . or, in this case, common land in the New Forest. The Royal Oak is a thatched hostelry that members of CAMRA will simply adore, the English pub at its best. Good beers tapped from the cask, unspoilt and basic bars, no food – just pickled eggs, high backed settles and pots and kettles hanging in a wide old chimney. You are welcome to bring your packed lunch to the pub to enjoy with your drink, with youngsters best-suited to the garden tables with their views of the Forest and its animals.

Just at the entrance to the Fritham car-park, you may notice a black, cylindrical object protruding from the ground. This is an old post-box, erected by the Schultze Gunpowder Factory that used to operate close to the former Groom's Lodge at nearby Eyeworth. It was originally constructed in the 19th century, and was renovated by the Forestry Commission in 1976. The post-box eased the postman's journey, saving him the ½ mile walk from Fritham to the factory. Mail was collected and delivered daily, excepting the Sabbath, with one old-penny being charged for letters and half an old-penny for newspapers.

Eyeworth Pond is a beautiful stretch of water, enjoying a perfect location amidst New Forest woodland. As well as attracting numerous wildfowl, the Pond acts as a magnet for the Forest's animals. It is a marvellous spectacle to see the local ponies wading into Eyeworth Pond, half-submerged in water, enjoying a cool bathe on a hot summer's day! The Pond, incidentally, also owes its existence to the Schultze Gunpowder Factory – the stream that runs through Howen Bottom was dammed to provide a water supply for the company. Just past the northern tip of Eyeworth Pond, the walk passes a well. This is shown on the OS sheets as 'Irons Well (Chalybeate)'. Chalybeate is defined in the dictionary as 'impregnated with iron salts'. The red coloration of the water makes this only too clear, as does the metallic taste for anybody brave enough to sample the waters!

Although short on miles, there are excellent opportunities for observing flora

Continued on page 20

17

Route 3

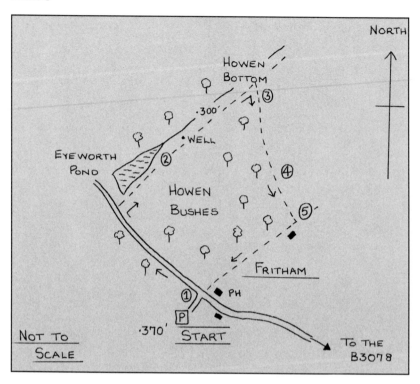

NORTH

HOWEN BOTTOM

③

·300'

• WELL

EYEWORTH POND

②

HOWEN BUSHES

④

⑤

FRITHAM

①

◆ PH

P

·370'   START

NOT TO SCALE

To THE B3078

Route 3

Fritham and Eyeworth Pond   **1.5 miles**

Start

Follow the B3078 eastwards from Fordingbridge for 7 miles, before turning right onto an unclassified road leading to Fritham. In the village, the public car-park lies just beyond the Royal Oak. GR 231141.

1. *Return to the road, and turn left to follow a lane downhill as far as Eyeworth Pond. Turn right, and follow the path alongside the pond.*

2. *Beyond the pond, the path passes through woodland – look out for Irons Well on the left-hand side – before emerging into open heath.*

3. *As soon as you emerge onto the heath, turn right and follow a grassy path (undefined) alongside the edge of the woodland. The path climbs gently towards an area of woodland 250 yards distant.*

4. *Continue in the same direction through these trees – again, no clearly defined path – for 100 yards to a cross-track.*

5. *Turn right, and follow the track back into Fritham, where you emerge alongside the Royal Oak.*

Public Transport

Wiltshire and Dorset Buses operate an infrequent service between Southampton and Fritham.

and fauna on this walk. The lane leading down from Fritham to Eyeworth Pond is lined with trees and bushes laden with berries and fruits in the late summer and early autumn – crab apples, holly, rowan, hawthorn, bramble, sloe and rose-hips to name but a few. Where the open heath borders Howens Bushes, I disturbed a grass-snake basking in the sun, whilst pigs often wander freely along the byways leading back to Fritham. Each day would present a different collection of species – the key is to walk quietly, to pause and to observe.

Refreshments
The Royal Oak lies at the end of the walk.

Eyeworth Pond

Linford Inclosure

Outline
Linford Bottom – Greenford Bottom – Great Linford Inclosure – Linford
Bottom.

Summary
A number of attractive streams flow through the hidden valleys of the Forest. This
2.5 mile circuit follows the banks of Linford Brook, a delightful river-bank stroll,
before returning through Great Linford Inclosure. The flora and fauna in the
neighbourhood make this a walk with exciting possibilities. The quiet, observant
visitor could stumble across the fallow deer that inhabit this corner of the Forest,
whilst the fallen oaks are home to a number of hornets' nests.

Attractions
Linford Brook is one of those meandering stretches of water, with its shallows and
deep pools, that forms an ever-popular attraction for children. Whether it be
paddling, fishing for minnows, water fights or more serious mini-beast hunts, it will
certainly prove difficult to persuade your youngsters that a walk is equally
rewarding! Along the river bank lie moss- and lichen-covered oaks, some of which
have fallen to provide nesting sites for hornets. The hornet is the largest member of
the wasp family in this country. Despite its fearsome reputation, it is in fact far less
angry than the humble wasp. The old hollow oaks of the New Forest provide the
perfect site for hornets' nests, where the queen can raise her offspring, none of
whom will survive the winter frosts. As with other wasps, only the queen survives
the winter.

The stream courses in mid-summer come alive with numerous dragonflies.
Species such as the common hawker apparently patrol their own patch, chasing off
rivals who retreat with torn wings from ferocious battles! Any smaller flying fry that
the dragonfly encounters will simply be devoured. July is generally the month when
the dragonfly emerges in full-flight along the river bank. The nymph will climb the
stem of a convenient water-loving plant, its skin will split and blood will course into
its wings to extend them. This is a spectacle, however, that you are more likely to
observe on a television documentary than in actuality.

Great Linford Inclosure is an area of mixed woodland, where mighty oaks stand
cheek by jowl with more modest conifers. This patch of the Forest was inclosed in
1846, since when many of its trees have reached maturity. It is known that fallow
deer inhabit quiet corners of the New Forest such as Linford Inclosure. Deer feed at
dawn and dusk, although you may be fortunate enough to disturb a resting creature
at other times. Deer are, however, extremely timid and will only be spotted by quiet,
patient visitors. Fallow deer display a seasonal pattern of activity. The rut takes
place in the autumn, when the master bucks fray the bark of saplings to mark

Continued on page 24

21

Route 4

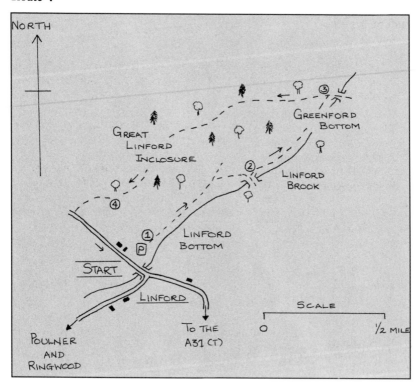

NORTH

GREAT
LINFORD
INCLOSURE

GREENFORD
BOTTOM

③

②

LINFORD
BROOK

④

①

P

LINFORD
BOTTOM

START

LINFORD

POULNER
AND
RINGWOOD

TO THE
A31 (T)

SCALE

0   ½ MILE

Route 4

Linford Inclosure   2.5 miles

Start

Follow the A31(T) eastwards from Ringwood for 2 miles before turning left onto an unclassified road signposted to Shobley and Linford. The Linford Bottom car-park lies 1 mile along this road, on the right-hand side. GR 181072.

1. *From the car-park, follow a gravel track alongside the inclosure for $\frac{1}{2}$ mile to a junction. Fork right to a footbridge across Linford Brook.*

2. *Do not cross this bridge, but turn left and follow Linford Brook upstream for another $\frac{1}{2}$ mile until you reach a clearing – Greenford Bottom – and a gravel track.*

3. *Turn left, and follow the track into Great Linford Inclosure. Follow the gravelled track through the inclosure for 1 mile until it eventually bears right to climb gently to a gate.*

4. *Leave Linford Inclosure and follow the path beyond through the bracken and gorse to a lane. Turn left, and follow this lane back down to the Linford Bottom car-park, passing a pair of houses en route.*

Public Transport

Wiltshire and Dorset Buses run a service from Ringwood to Poulner, 1 mile from the start of the walk.

territory; male antlers are cast in April, at which point the buck displays his apparent embarrassment by becoming something of a recluse; mid-June sees the summer coats and broad-bladed antlers appearing, as well as the birth of fawns.

Refreshments
There are no refreshment facilities on this walk, other than a seasonal ice-cream vendor in the Linford Bottom car-park. The banks of Linford Brook provide excellent picnicking opportunities.

Linford Bottom

24

The Rufus Stone

Outline
Rufus Stone – Stricknage Wood – Coalmeer Gutter – Upper Canterton – Rufus Stone.

Summary
The Rufus Stone marks the spot where William II, son of the Conqueror, met his death under what today would be described as 'suspicious circumstances'. This short circuit explores the woods, Forest lawns and heathland around the Rufus Stone. An added attraction is the 'Walter Tyrell' – one of the Forest's ancient inns with a great sense of history.

Attractions
William II, the son of William the Conqueror, earned the nickname 'Rufus' on account of a shock of flaming red hair. The Rufus stone marks the spot where he was mysteriously killed. The commemorative marker is plain enough:

> "Here stood the oak tree on which an arrow
> shot by Sir Walter Tyrell at a stag glanced
> and struck King William II surnamed Rufus on
> the breast, of which he instantly died on the
> second day of August anno 1100.
> King William II being thus slain was laid on a
> cart belonging to one Purkess and drawn from
> hence to Winchester, and buried in the cathedral
> church of that city."

Case closed? Unfortunately not. Some experts have suggested that William's death was far from an accident. He was a dreadfully unpopular man, being physically ugly with a character to match. His brother Henry was a member of that ill-fated hunting party. Within 3 days he had been crowned as William's successor, against a back-drop of protests from one William de Breneuil. Breneuil was rightfully trying to claim the throne for Henry's elder brother Robert, Duke of Normandy, who at the time of Rufus' death was conveniently out of the country on a crusade. The plot thickens!

The walk passes through Stricknage Wood, an ancient patch of woodland filled with beech, oak and holly. In the heart of the wood, our steps follow Coalmeer Gutter. Do not be put off by such an appendage, however! The streams of the New Forest enjoy a number of names – in the south of the Forest they are called "waters", whereas here in the north the streams are called "gutters" and "brooks".

Where the walk emerges from Stricknage Wood into a clearing, sharp-eyed visitors may well glimpse a spotted flycatcher. This summer visitor likes nothing

Continued on page 28

Route 5

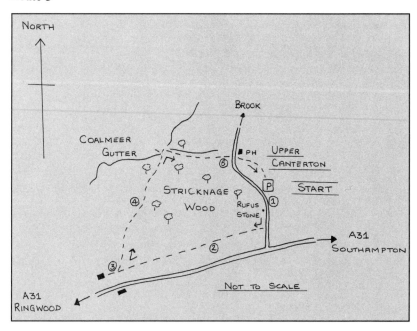

NORTH

BROOK

COALMEER GUTTER

PH

UPPER CANTERTON

⑤

START

STRICKNAGE WOOD

P

RUFUS STONE

①

④

②

A31 SOUTHAMPTON

③

NOT TO SCALE

A31 RINGWOOD

Route 5

The Rufus Stone   2 miles

Start

2 miles before the A31(T) joins the M27 at Cadnam, an unclassified road heads northwards to Upper Canterton and the Rufus Stone. There is a car-park alongside the Rufus Stone site. GR 271125.

1. *Walk back up the road in the direction of the A31(T) for 300 yards to a wooden barrier on the right-hand side. Turn right, and follow the track ahead, bearing right at the first fork.*

2. *Continue across the open heath for $\frac{1}{2}$ mile, until you approach an old white-washed house. There are many tracks across the hilltop – the best approach is to keep walking in a westerly direction, parallel to the A31, which lies about 100 yards to your left. Try and look out for one main gravel track to follow.*

3. *100 yards before you reach the house, turn right and follow a path through a number of holly trees to reach an area of open heath. Follow this path downhill, heading for the trees ahead. The path subsequently borders the woodland – on your right – before entering the trees.*

4. *The path passes through Stricknage Wood before reaching Coalmeer Gutter at the bottom of the valley. Turn right here, and follow a path that runs parallel to the stream before emerging into a clearing. Turn right and follow the track that crosses this clearing until you reach the Walter Tyrrell Inn.*

5. *Cross the road alongside the pub, and follow the gravelled track to the right of the red-brick cottage. This track bears right in front of a thatched cottage to return you to the Rufus Stone car-park.*

Public Transport

Wiltshire and Dorset Buses operate a Southampton to Lyndhurst service that passes through Castle Malwood, less than 1 mile from the Rufus Stone.

better than an open glade in the heart of woodland. It attracts attention by its sallies into the air after flying insects, always returning to the same perch or post. Here it will sit upright with its rather long tail held downward, waiting for its next flycatching sortie. The spotted flycatcher is readily identified – grey-brown above with spots on the head, near white beneath with faint streaks on the breast, and 5 inches long.

Refreshments
Almost at the end of the walk, you will pass the Walter Tyrell Inn. This excellent pub offers a fine selection of food for all members of the family, as well as providing a play-area for children.

Forest cottage at Upper Canterton

The Knightwood Oak and Holidays Hill Inclosure

Outline
Knightwood Oak – Warwick Slade – The Reptiliary – Holidays Hill – Holidays Hill Inclosure – The Knightwood Oak.

Summary
The Knightwood Oak is perhaps the most famous tree in the Forest, being arguably both the oldest and largest example of *Quercus robur*. The Knightwood Oak lies alongside the Bolderwood Ornamental Drive, a collection of conifers from around the world that were planted over 150 years ago. In addition to these highlights, this short circuit explores Holidays Hill, an inclosure that dates back to 1676. In the midst of this ancient woodland lies the Reptiliary, a collection of the Forest's reptiles that are all-too-often elusive in their natural environment.

Attractions
The Knightwood Oak is thought to be over 400 years old, which makes it one of the oldest trees in the New Forest. Its 21-foot girth is certainly unsurpassed by any other Forest oak. The information board alongside the Knightwood Oak attributes its great age to the practice of 'pollarding'. This word is derived from the French word 'poil' which is translated 'to behead'. The limbs of the tree were removed at regular intervals, leaving a permanent trunk from which new shoots would appear. This supply of timber could be used for a variety of purposes that ranged from animal fodder through to fencing material.

Around the Knightwood Oak is an enclosure named the 'Monarch's Grove'. This contains 18 smaller oaks planted by Elizabeth II on the 12th of April 1979. Each oak commemorates a visit to the Forest by a reigning monarch. Chronologically, the roll of honour runs William I, William II, Henry I, Henry II, John, Henry III, Edward I, Edward III, Richard II, Henry VII, Henry VIII, Edward VI, James I, Charles I, Charles II, James II, George III and Edward VII. The great attraction of the Forest was naturally its fine hunting. To mark Elizabeth II's visit in 1979, two further trees were planted nearby. Both the Queen's Oak and the Edinburgh Oak are passed near the start of the walk. Their diminutive size illustrates the slow growth of *Quercus robur*, and provides clear evidence of the Knightwood Oak's great age.

The New Forest, with its ponds, heathland and bogs, is a paradise for reptiles. Unfortunately for the visitor, reptiles are very elusive creatures, in part due to their camouflage, in part due to their natural shyness. To provide an insight into this aspect of the Forest, the Forestry Commission have created a reptiliary on Holidays Hill. This is a series of open concrete enclosures, where each reptile's favourite habitat has been re-created. The various species on display include grass and smooth snakes, adders, sand and common lizards, newts, toads and slow worms.

Continued on page 32

29

Route 6

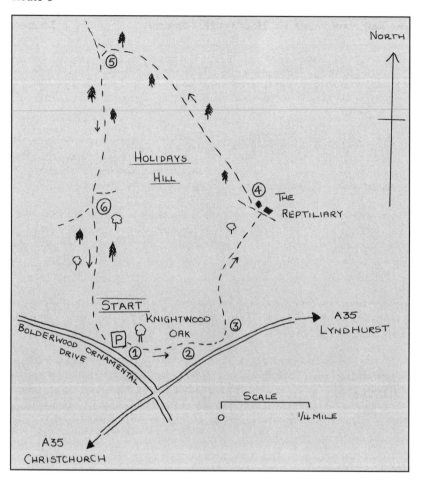

NORTH

HOLIDAYS
HILL

⑤

⑥

④ THE
REPTILIARY

START

KNIGHTWOOD
OAK

P ① ②

③

A35
LYNDHURST

BOLDERWOOD ORNAMENTAL DRIVE

A35
CHRISTCHURCH

SCALE

0   ¼ MILE

Route 6

The Knightwood Oak and Holidays Hill Inclosure   2.5 miles

Start

The Knightwood Oak parking area lies just north of the A35, 3 miles south-west of Lyndhurst. As you approach the area, an unclassified road is signposted as 'Bolderwood Ornamental Drive'. The car-park lies 300 yards along this turning. GR 264064.

1. *Follow the path out of the far end of the car-park. Shortly, you will pass the Queen's Oak and the Edinburgh Oak on the right of the path, with the Knightwood Oak away on the left in its enclosure. Where the gravelled path bears to the left to the Knightwood Oak, continue straight ahead along a grassy path to a gate.*

2. *The path leaves the woodland at this gate and bears to the right towards a second gate and the A35. Cross towards the main road but, before you reach the gate, bear left along a grassy path that leads down to a waterway labelled as 'Warwickslade Cutting' on the OS sheet. A wooden footbridge crosses this watercourse just before the A35.*

3. *Once across this footbridge, bear left across the heath, following an obvious path away from the A35. In close-on $\frac{1}{2}$ mile, this path brings you to Holidays Hill Cottage and the Reptiliary.*

4. *A gravelled forestry road passes to the left of the Reptiliary into the coniferous woodland beyond. Follow this track up to the top of Holidays Hill until, some $\frac{1}{2}$ mile distant, it reaches a distinct junction alongside a triangular green.*

5. *Fork left at this green to head back towards the car-park. Continue downhill for $\frac{1}{2}$ mile, ignoring all left and right turns, until at the foot of the slope the path levels out. Before the main track bears right, there are two footpaths branching off to the left.*

6. *Take the second of these left turns, a grassy footpath through the trees. It crosses a small stream (ideal for paddling!) before returning to the car-park.*

Public Transport

The X1 Southampton, Lyndhurst and Bournemouth bus service, passes along the A35 just minutes from the start of the walk. Ask for Knightwood Oak (Burley Lodge Turn). Service operated by Wiltshire and Dorset Buses.

Youngsters will find 'reptile spotting' at the reptiliary an engaging occupation. What initially appears to be a twig or a piece of foliage, can well turn out to be something far more interesting!

Refreshments
This walk lies in the heart of the Forest, where cafes and pubs are thankfully non-existent! A picnic in the Forest is a most pleasant alternative.

Tree frog habitat, The Reptiliary.

Dur Hill Down and Whitten Pond

Outline
Burbush Hill car-park – Dur Hill Inclosure – Dur Hill Down – Whitten Pond – Burbush Hill car-park.

Summary
Dur Hill Down is quite simply one of the greatest expanses of natural heath on the forest. There are no 'honey-pot' attractions on the Down, simply the natural flora and fauna that make the heathlands such a unique habitat. The Down is also a fine vantage point, with expansive views across the surrounding areas of the New Forest. Two further features on the route are the remains of the disused Brockenhurst to Ringwood railway, and Whitten Pond.

Attractions
Dur Hill Down, a mile or so south of Burley, is a fine expanse of natural heath. Lowland heath has disappeared at an alarming rate this century, partly due to the plough and partly due to building and construction. The New Forest is one of the few areas in the country where sufficient heathland exists to support the full range of associated flora and fauna.

The heathland in the Forest is known to be one of the last strongholds for many threatened species. Whilst sightings cannot be guaranteed, it is known that the Forest heaths support birds such as the woodlark, the Dartford warbler, the night-jar and the stonechat, as well as reptiles that include the sand lizard and the smooth snake. Butterflies are another feature of the heaths, with the silver-studded blue and the grayling being but two unusual species.

The dictionary defines a heath as 'an area of flattish uncultivated land with low shrubs'. The shrubs that predominate on Dur Hill are heather and gorse. There are in fact three types of heather. Bell heather is named after its beautiful crimson bells, that flower towards the end of June. The pink-flowered, cross-leaved heather grows in wet hollows, and is recognisable by its grey leaves. The most common heather on the open heaths is the ling – or Scottish heather. Its rose-purple flowers bring a delightful splash of colour to Dur Hill Down in August. Coincidentally, three strains of gorse exist. The Dwarf and Welsh varieties are outnumbered by the more humble common gorse. This strong-growing shrub, up to six feet in height, is found in abundance on the open heathland.

Refreshments
There are no refreshment facilities on the walk itself. The village of Burley, a mile north of the Burbush Hill Parking Area, has several pubs and tea-rooms. Towards the end of the walk, the footpath passes Whitten Pond, whose banks provide excellent picnicking spots.

Route 7

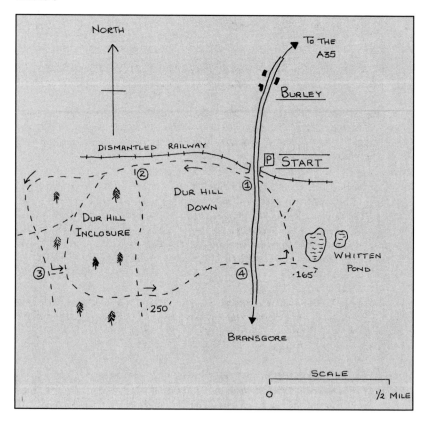

NORTH

TO THE A35

BURLEY

DISMANTLED RAILWAY

② DUR HILL DOWN

P START ①

DUR HILL INCLOSURE

③ ④

·165

WHITTEN POND

·250

BRANSGORE

SCALE

0   ½ MILE

34

Route 7

Dur Hill Down and Whitten Pond   3.5 miles

Start

1-mile south of Burley, on the Bransgore road, the Burbush Hill car-park lies just off the road alongside the disused Ringwood to Brockenhurst railway. GR 203018.

1. *Return to the Burley road, cross the railway bridge and turn immediately right. Follow the path ahead that runs parallel to the old trackbed, along the northern edge of Dur Hill Down. In ½ mile, you will reach the north-eastern corner of Dur Hill Inclosure.*

2. *Continue ahead along the northern edge of the inclosure, ignoring any left-turns into the woods, the sandy path overshadowed by some majestic pine trees. At the far end of Dur Hill Inclosure, the path bears left to continue along the inclosure's western boundary. The path climbs and descends a short, sharp hill before reaching a cross-track in a dip. Continue straight ahead to the top of the next climb, where you negotiate the fence on the left (no stile) to secure a grassy ride that leads into Dur Hill Inclosure.*

3. *Follow this ride for a short distance to a T-junction. Bear right, and follow the gravelled forestry road through to the eastern edge of the inclosure, ignoring all side turns. Continue following the main gravelled forestry road across Dur Hill Down to the Burley road.*

4. *Continue following a footpath on the opposite side of the road across the heath to Whitten Pond. Just before the pond, a path turns off on the left to head across the open heath and back to the Burbush Hill car-park. En route, fork left at the only junction.*

Public Transport

The Ringwood to Burley, Bransgore and Poole buses, run by Wiltshire and Dorset Buses, pass the car-park.

Map reading at Whitten Pond

Burley and Turf Hill

Outline

Burley – Turf Hill – Holmsley Old Station – Scrape Bottom – Clay Hill – Burley

Summary

This exhilarating walk explores the open heathland to the east of Burley, one of the Forest's prettiest villages. The fine Forest panorama afforded from the hilltop locations disguises the fact that in the valleys lie any number of ancient smugglers' paths. In years gone by, it was a case of 'all roads leading to Burley', with the village serving as a distribution centre for contraband. A more recent attraction is the trackbed of the disused Ringwood to Brockenhurst railway, which now serves as an excellent footpath.

Attractions

Burley is one of the prettiest villages in the Forest, with strong associations with hunting and horseriding. In the past, the village was known throughout the region for its smuggling connections. Many tracks and pathways led from the nearby coast to the village, where the Queen's Head served as an important distribution centre for smuggled liquor and other contraband. The inn allegedly dates back to 1699, with low ceilings and beams adding a touch of historic authenticity. A few years ago, a hidden cellar was discovered beneath the Queen's Head. Its contents should come as no surprise – pistols, bottles and old coins.

The disused Ringwood to Brockenhurst railway is followed for just over one mile of this walk. Various features of interest to railway enthusiasts occur along this section of the track. Just a couple of hundred yards along this part of the line, we pass an old level-crossing keeper's cottage alongside an unclassified lane leading to Burley. In Holmsley, the old station platforms are still intact, whilst the station-master's house now serves as 'The Old Station Tea House'. The railway was built in 1847 and was operating until 1964, although in its latter years it offered nothing other than irregular freight services.

The section of track-bed followed on this walk passes through a damp, low-lying area marked on the OS sheet as Holmsley Bog. The bogs in the Forest are formed of extensive deposits of saturated peat that has accumulated in hollows and valleys. According to the experts, these bogs represent some of the finest examples of their kind in Western Europe. Along their watercourses are found alder and willow carr, whilst the rich flora extends to such species as the marsh gentian and the bog orchid. The insect life includes the tiny damsel fly and the large marsh grasshopper, whilst the damp environment attracts lapwing, redshank, curlew, snipe and other marsh birds. The railway line passes through the marshland on a raised embankment, providing extensive views of this unique habitat.

Continued on page 40

Route 8

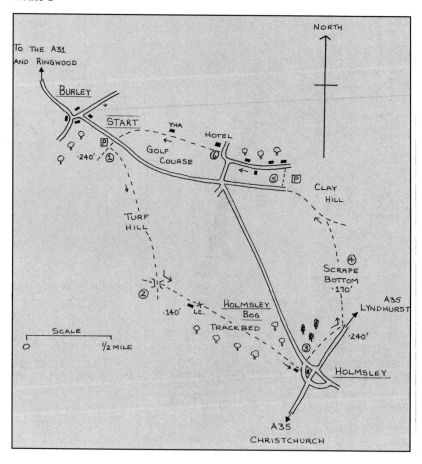

Route 8

Burley and Turf Hill   4.5 miles

Start

Burley lies 4 miles south-east of Ringwood. Take the A31 Southampton road out of Ringwood for 2 miles, before turning right onto an unclassified road leading into Burley. Leave the village on the Lymington road, and in just 250 yards you will find a car-park on the right-hand side. This is opposite the village school and the adjoining cricket pitch. GR 214028.

1. *From the car-park, take the footpath which heads parallel to the road onto the open heathland. Two short wooden posts mark the start of the path as it leaves the track leading from the Burley road to the car-park. This path very quickly bears to the right across Turf Hill before dropping down to the trackbed of the old Brockenhurst railway at Greenberry Bridge.*

2. *Scramble down to the trackbed and head eastwards for 1 mile, across Holmsley Bog and onto the old Holmsley Station site. The trackbed beyond the station has been severed by a new road. Cross the stile just past the platform onto this road, turn left for 20 yards to the junction with the Burley to Brockenhurst road, and cross over to a stile in the overgrown hedgerow opposite. Follow the path beyond this stile for a few yards to a crosstrack.*

3. *Cross straight over and follow the narrow path ahead as it climbs to run parallel to the A35 on the right-hand side. In less than $\frac{1}{2}$ mile, at the top of a climb, a gateway on the right leads out onto the A35. At this point, our path bears to the left and descends into Scrape Bottom.*

4. *The path climbs out of Scrape Bottom, climbing the opposite hillside, before bearing to the right to join a wide grassy ride. Turn left, and follow this ride as far as the Clay Hill car-park and a lane leading back into Burley.*

5. *Just past the car-park, turn right onto a path that crosses the heath to reach the cottages and woodland ahead. Turn left along the lane in front of these cottages and, in 300 yards, turn right at a junction.*

6. *In just a few yards, in front of the White Buck Hotel, turn left into Cott Lane. This lane leads past the local youth hostel and golf course, before emerging onto the Burley road. The car-park lies on the opposite side of the road.*

The paths that pass through Scrape Bottom are some of the historic sunken ways used by smugglers in years gone by. Cargoes were landed on the coast at Lymington, Milford and Milton, before being carried throughout the Forest. Lymington was vividly described by Daniel Defoe in 1727. He maintained that the port engaged in no foreign trade 'except it be what we call smuggling and roguing; which, I may say, is the reigning commerce of all this part of the English coast.' The contraband was extensive – tea, tobacco, brandy, spices and wines being the most frequently smuggled items. The punishment for convicted smugglers was severe, and included transportation and even hanging. The Naked Man (see walk 9) was one natural gallows provided by the Forest's great trees.

Refreshments
The historic Queen's Head in Burley offers a wide choice of food, as well as making provision for children. The Old Station Tea House at Holmsley lies conveniently at the walk's halfway point.

Public Transport
Wiltshire and Dorset Buses operate a Southampton to Bournemouth and Poole service which passes the Queen's Head in Burley.

Burley village

Wilverley Inclosure and the Naked Man

Outline
Wilverley Plain – Wilverley Inclosure – The Naked Man – Wilverley Plain.

Summary
A beautiful walk that encompasses both open heathland and forest inclosure. Wilverley Plain provides excellent grazing for local ponies and cattle, whilst the inclosure is an area of mixed woodland criss-crossed by a network of generally level paths. An added attraction is the Naked Man, the remains of a once great oak tree that served as a natural gallows.

Attractions
Wilverley Inclosure dates back to the second half of the 18th century, although the original attempts to create this area of mixed woodland ended in failure. A subsequent planting in 1809 proved more successful, with many of the oak trees bordering the car-park being original specimens. The trees within the plantation range from the oak, beech and birch, through to various firs and pine trees. Commercial felling is confined to the winter months to avoid disturbing nesting birds and other wildlife. Youngsters armed with their I-Spy Trees booklet will soon be heading towards the Award of Merit!

A rich variety of bird life can be seen within the inclosure. The majestic oak tree is known to support several hundred invertebrates, which in turn attract species such as nuthatches and treecreepers to the forest. The treecreeper, with its long, thin and curved bill, is ideally suited for investigating the food potential of cracks in the bark of a tree. Its diet consists almost entirely of the eggs, pupae, larvae, and adults of insects and spiders. The nuthatch enjoys wider-ranging tastes, being equally partial to the occasional tree fruit or nut.

The Naked Man has clearly seen better days. This decaying tree stump is a pale shadow of its former glory as a majestic oak, but it has been preserved as a reminder of its former status – a natural gallows. The Forest's highwaymen and smugglers would be strung from its boughs as a salutary reminder of the consequences of trafficking in contraband. The Naked Man stands alongside a track that ran from the coast to the village of Burley, where the Queen's Head Inn was a smuggler's haunt. Its location could not have been more opportune. The name, incidentally, derives from a period in the tree's history when its more substantial boughs formed a silhouette of a ghostly naked figure.

Refreshments
At the end of the walk, Wilverley Plain provides a fine spot for a picnic. There are, in fact, a number of picnic tables alongside the parking area. Back on the A35, the Old Station Tea House at Holmsley serves delicious cream teas.

Route 9

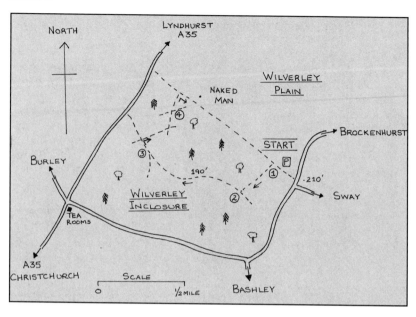

Route 9

Wilverley Inclosure and the Naked Man

2 miles

Start

Wilverley Inclosure borders the A35 approximately 6 miles south-west of Lyndhurst. When approaching the area from Lyndhurst, the main A35 is crossed by the unclassified Burley to Brockenhurst road. Turn left towards Brockenhurst and, a short distance past the turning to Sway, park in the Wilverley Inclosure car-park. GR 254010.

1. *Walk to the far end of the parking area and pass through the gate on the left-hand side into Wilverley Inclosure. Follow the main gravelled track ahead for 600 yards to a T-junction, ignoring the various side turns.*

2. *Turn right, and follow another gravelled track for well over $\frac{1}{2}$ mile. Towards the end of this section of the walk, the path descends into a small valley. 200 yards on from the top of the subsequent rise, a wide gravelled ride joins the path on the left-hand side.*

3. *Continue ahead at this junction for just 50 yards to a crosstrack. Turn right onto a grassy path, which is followed for 350 yards to another crosstrack in the middle of a clearing. Follow the path to the left for 50 yards to another crosstrack.*

4. *Cross straight over and follow the path ahead through dense tree cover for 300 yards to a gate. Leave the inclosure, and follow the path to the right for $\frac{3}{4}$ mile back to the parking area. To your left lies Wilverley Plain, fine open common grazed by Forest ponies, whilst the sad looking tree stump passed en route is all that remains of the Naked Man!*

Public Transport

Wiltshire and Dorset Buses operate a Summer Sunday service between Lymington, Lyndhurst and Ringwood which passes close to Wilverley Inclosure.

The Naked Man

Ober Water

Outline
Puttles Bridge car-park – Ober Water – Alridge Hill Inclosure – Ober Water – Whitefield Moor – Puttles Bridge car-park.

Summary
Brockenhurst – literally 'Badgers Wood' – is a picturesque Forest village with a timeless feel. Although criss-crossed by modern communications such as the A337 and the main Bournemouth railway, the local ponies still graze on the village green as their ancestors did in centuries past. A mile or so to the west of the village lies Ober Water, a delightful Forest stream tinged rusty-brown by the local peaty soils. This short walk explores the river-bank, as well as neighbouring areas of heath and woodland. A quite superb short walk that even very young children could manage.

Attractions
Ober Water is one of those rivers that naturally appeals to youngsters. The water is easily accessible, and its shallow depth makes it ideal for paddling. Furthermore, the smooth gravel that covers the river bed means that parents will not face the prospect of muddy legs! The gravel is somewhat puzzling. The local soils hereabouts are peaty, hence the brown coloration of Ober Water. Quite where the gravels come from is one of the problems that occupies the minds of geographers. They are actually Ice Age deposits that have been washed down from the flat-topped Forest plateau some 5 miles to the west. Despite the water's brown tint, it is extremely clear. Spotting the many shoals of minnows that swim up-and-down the river will certainly amuse young children.

Alridge Hill Inclosure is but one of the many inclosures in the New Forest. Their history dates back many centuries. From the Middle Ages onwards, there was a vast demand for timber in England. Much of the wood was used for shipbuilding, with large quantities of Forest timber being used at nearby shipbuilding centres such as Bucklers Hard. The problem came when seeking to replenish tree stocks. Grazing deer and the Commoners' livestock would very quickly devour young seedlings. This gave rise to the inclosures, such as the one on Alridge Hill. The Alridge Hill Inclosure dates back to 1681, although most of today's trees only date back to a replanting after the First World War.

Just before reaching the Whitefield car-park, the walk passes the borders of Whitefield Moor. This vast area of closely cropped turf was actually heathland until the last war. To ensure adequate wartime food supplies, 1,000 acres of Forest heath was ploughed up and planted with cereals and potatoes. In the immediate post-war years, the land was reseeded with clover and grasses to form fine pasture. This type of grassland does not develop naturally on the Forest's poor soils. It is not surprising to discover large numbers of cattle, ponies and donkeys grazing on Whitefield Moor.

Route 10

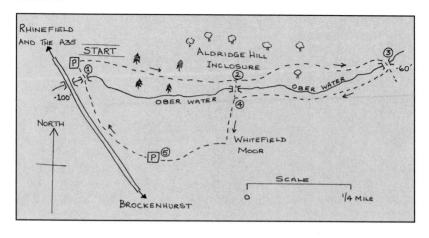

Route 10

Ober Water   1.5 miles

Start

The Puttle's Bridge car-park lies 1½ miles west of Brockenhurst on the unclassified road leading to the Rhinefield Ornamental Drive. GR 272029.

1. *Continue eastwards along the path leading out of the car-park. This gravelled right-of-way reaches a wooden footbridge in just under ½ mile. (Cross the bridge if you want a short walk, and rejoin the route at point 4.)*

2. *Continue along the northern bank of Ober Water for close on ½ mile to a second wooden footbridge. The path forks en route – bear left along the gravelled path away from the river bank, to pass through the edge of Alridge Hill Inclosure.*

3. *Cross Ober Water and immediately bear right to follow the river bank back to the first footbridge, ignoring the more obvious gravel path that heads away from the river.*

4. *At the footbridge, follow the gravelled path to the left that heads away from Ober Water and up towards Whitefield Moor. Pass through a gap in the hedgerow just before the Moor, and turn right to follow the hedgerow through to the Whitefield Moor car-park.*

5. *Pass through this parking area and follow the gravelled path back down to Puttle's Bridge car-park. To return to the parking-area involves crossing a footbridge across Ober Water.*

Public Transport

Brockenhurst, just a mile or so from the start of the walk, lies on the railway line between Southampton and Bournemouth.

Refreshments

Hungry visitors will find pubs and cafes just a mile from the start of the walk in Brockenhurst. The river-bank alongside Puttle's Bridge car-park provides a number of fine picnic spots.

Lyndhurst war memorial

Lyndhurst and Longwater Lawn

Outline

Bolton's Bench – The Ridge – Longwater Lawn – Mallard Wood –
Bolton's Bench.

Summary

Lyndhurst is widely recognised as the "Capital of the New Forest", the seat of the ancient Court of Verderers from where justice has traditionally been administered in the Forest. This beautiful walk to the east of the town contains all of the elements for which the New Forest is so well-known – heathland, woodland, lawn and stream. The rural tranquility offers the perfect antidote to the unfortunately traffic-clogged streets in Lyndhurst.

Attractions

Lyndhurst has been the centre of administration in the New Forest since the 14th century. A Verderers' Court has sat in the town for many centuries, and to this day any local resident can make a 'presentment' on one Monday in every two months. The Court's sessions in the Verderers' Hall are open to the public, with issues relating to commoners' rights being the most usual topic of discussion on the agenda.

Lyndhurst is also home to the New Forest Museum and Visitor Centre. This is *the* place to visit for anyone new to the Forest and its attractions. As well as "The Changing Forest" audio visual show, a montage of hundreds of photographs showing the Forest through the seasons, there are also local displays that feature such attractions as the famous New Forest Embroidery, and Brusher Mills the legendary snake-catcher! Adjoining the museum (entry fee) is an extensive tourist information centre dispensing a vast number of free leaflets.

The walk sets off from Bolton's Bench, named after Lord Bolton a Lord Warden of the Forest in 1688. The bench, a fine viewpoint, surrounds a clump of yew trees that adorn an ancient mound. The site is possibly a burial mound dating back to the Iron Age. If you are bringing youngsters to the area in mid-winter, don't forget the family toboggan. The slopes around Bolton's Bench provide arguably the best tobogganing in the New Forest.

Beyond Bolton's Bench, the walk initially borders a linear earthwork labelled on the OS sheet as 'The Ridge'. This interesting landmark dates back to the 13th century, when 200 acres of the Forest were encircled in order to provide a royal deer park. This hunting ground was replaced in 1670 by Charles II, when a 'New Park' was created near Brockenhurst. North of the Ridge, the circuit eventually emerges onto Longwater Lawn. These 'lawns' are beautiful areas of grassland dotted around the Forest, where the turf has been closely cropped by the local ponies and

Continued on page 52

Route 11

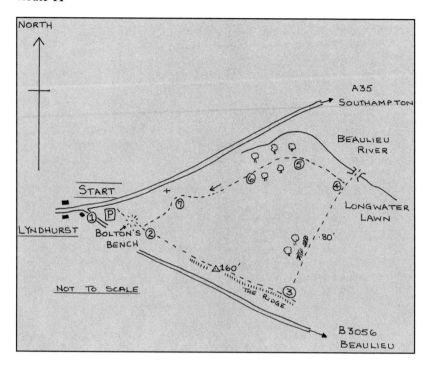

NORTH

A35
SOUTHAMPTON

BEAULIEU
RIVER

START

LYNDHURST

BOLTON'S
BENCH

LONGWATER
LAWN

NOT TO SCALE

△160'
THE RIDGE

B3056
BEAULIEU

50

Route 11

Lyndhurst and Longwater Lawn   3 miles

Start

Bolton's Bench car-park lies on the eastern edge of Lyndhurst, alongside the junction of the A35 Southampton road with the B3056 Beaulieu road. GR 305082.

1. *Climb to the wooded summit of Bolton's Bench to enjoy one of the Forest's best views. Descend to the metalled drive below that passes to the left of the local cricket square. Where this drive bears left to the cemetery, continue straight ahead along a stony track through a parking area.*

2. *Beyond the parking area, the track continues across the heath. After passing a trig point on the right-hand side – worth the detour for the view – continue ahead for $\frac{3}{4}$ mile until a distinct path heads off on the left-hand side. To check your location, the view to the right at this point looks across the B3056 to an hotel in the distance.*

3. *Turn left, and follow this well-defined track towards a small group of coniferous trees some 300 yards ahead. The path passes to the right of these trees, before emerging onto Longwater Lawn. Ahead is a footbridge across the infant Beaulieu River.*

4. *Instead of crossing the bridge, bear sharp left just before the river and follow a wide grassy ride through the trees to a second wooden footbridge. Beyond this bridge, walk in the same direction towards the woodland ahead. When you reach the nearest corner of the woods, walk down its right-hand edge for 30 yards until a path on the left enters the trees.*

5. *Follow the path through the woods for $\frac{1}{2}$ mile. On the far side of the trees, you emerge onto the heathland with the busy A35 road 100 yards or so away on the right-hand side.*

6. *Dozens of paths – not marked on the OS sheets – head back to Lyndhurst! Intuition is needed! Continue ahead on paths of your choice, keeping a parallel course to the A35. Before too long, a clump of massive pine trees appears on the horizon $\frac{1}{2}$ mile ahead. Beat a course for this landmark.*

7. *Lyndhurst Cemetery lies just beyond the pine trees. Follow the cemetery boundary fence to the left until Bolton's Bench comes into view. It is then just a short walk past the cricket pitch to the car-park.*

donkeys. Longwater Lawn enjoys a picturesque aspect, with its fine pasture and the headwaters of the Beaulieu River drawing in large numbers of local livestock.

Refreshments
Lyndhurst's High Street lies just minutes from the end of the walk. Here you will find excellent pubs, such as the Stag Inn and the Mailman's Arms, as well as cafes, such as the Court House Tea-rooms.

Public Transport
Buses from Southampton to both Lymington and Bournemouth pass through Lyndhurst. The services are operated by Wiltshire and Dorset Buses.

Bolton's Bench

Route 12 3 miles
Beaulieu Road and Denny Wood

Outline
Shatterford car-park – Woodfidley Passage – Denny Wood – Shatterford
Bottom – Shatterford car-park.

Summary
Beaulieu Road is little more than a halt on the Southampton to Bournemouth
railway that serves the nearby Beaulieu Road Hotel. All around is nothing but
heath and wooded forest. Five times each year, however, Beaulieu Road takes on a
carnival atmosphere as dealers gather for the New Forest Pony Sales. This 3-mile
walk explores the area to the south-west of Beaulieu Road, where further
attractions include Bishop's Dyke and areas of exceptional New Forest bog. The
paths are generally level, with no strenuous climbs involved.

Attractions
To the north of the B3056, opposite Beaulieu Road Station, the motley collection of
wooden enclosures, platforms and auction rings could almost be taken from a scene
in a western movie. This is actually the site of the New Forest Pony Sales, held on
five occasions each year. For one day in each of the months April, August,
September, October and November, hundreds of dealers converge on this lonely
spot. Romany traders stand side-by-side with parents looking for their child's first
pony. The trading follows a set pattern, with foals being traded in the morning, and
horses and adult ponies in the afternoon.

The 'Civil Parish' is the smallest unit of government within the United
Kingdom, having powers over expenditure items such as the village hall roof or a
park bench. This walk is contained within the boundaries of 'Denny Lodge CP', the
largest parish by area within the United Kingdom. Denny Lodge CP extends from
Matley Heath near Ashurst as far as King's Copse Inclosure near Fawley, a
distance of some 6 miles. The population of the parish, however, is a mere 500
persons. Denny Lodge itself is a former Groom Keeper's residence, located a few
miles south-east of Lyndhurst. Today it serves as a Head Forester's residence.

The OS Outdoor Leisure map shows this walk cutting through, as well as
running parallel to, a medieval earthwork known as 'Bishop's Dyke'. The dyke was
constructed in 1284 at the behest of John de Pontoise, Bishop of Winchester. The
logic behind the enclosure of 500 acres of boggy wasteland is something of a puzzle,
although its potential to attract wildfowl would have made this area of marsh quite
useful as a hunting ground. Local folklore alleges that the king allowed Bishop John
to enclose that area of land that he could crawl around in the space of one day!

Bogs have developed across the New Forest in the permanently wet sites such as
low-lying heathland. An outstanding example of a New Forest bog is found at
Shatterford Bottom, just before the end of the walk. These bogs comprise in the

Continued on page 56

53

Route 12

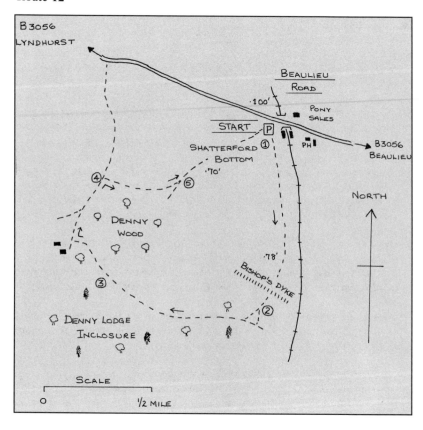

B3056
LYNDHURST

BEAULIEU
ROAD

·100'

PONY
SALES

START   P

B3056
BEAULIEU

SHATTERFORD ①
BOTTOM
·70'

PH

④

⑤

NORTH

DENNY
WOOD

·78'

BISHOP'S DYKE

③

②

DENNY LODGE
INCLOSURE

SCALE

0   ½ MILE

54

Route 12

Beaulieu Road and Denny Wood   3 miles

Start

Beaulieu Road Station lies 3 miles east of Lyndhurst on the B3056 Beaulieu road. Just to the west of the station, park in the Shatterford car-park. GR 348064.

1. *From Shatterford car-park, head south along a sandy track that runs parallel to the railway. Keep straight on along this track for 1 mile until you reach the borders of Denny Lodge Inclosure, crossing areas of marshland en route.*

2. *Pass directly through a clump of silver birch trees to reach a crosstrack, 50 yards before a gateway that leads into the inclosure. Turn right before the gateway and follow the path through open woodland and heath, and across marshland, for $\frac{3}{4}$ mile. Just beyond a pair of footbridges, the path enters Denny Wood.*

3. *Pass directly through the woodland ahead. The path soon borders an open field on the left before emerging onto the driveway leading to Denny Lodge. Turn right. In $\frac{1}{4}$ mile, at the foot of a small dip, you will reach a lopped tree-trunk and a single-bar wooden barrier on the right-hand side. Cross over the barrier, or walk around it.*

4. *Turn right along a woodland path. In a short distance, you reach a clearing caused by storm damage. Bear left in this clearing and follow the path through the trees and out onto the open heath. Two hundred yards ahead, you reach a T-junction.*

5. *Turn left, and follow the well-defined path across the heath back to the distinct clump of trees that surrounds the Shatterford car-park. Just before the end of the walk, a footbridge takes the path across Shatterford Bottom, another extensive area of marshland.*

Public Transport

Trains running between Southampton and Bournemouth occasionally stop at Beaulieu Road, just minutes from the start of the walk. Wiltshire and Dorset Buses run a Sunday Rider service between Lymington and Lyndhurst, which passes Beaulieu Road.

main deposits of saturated peat, which has accumulated in the forest's hollows. It is possible that a bearded David Bellamy look-alike will be spotted in the depths of Shatterford Bottom, on the lookout for the area's outstanding flora and fauna. This could well include marsh gentian, bog orchid, damsel fly, large marsh grasshopper, lapwing, redshank and snipe. Certainly, Western Europe has few bogland sites that can better those found in the New Forest.

Refreshments
Across the railway line from the Shatterford car-park lies the Beaulieu Road Pub. This fine old inn, as well as welcoming families, offers a good selection of traditional pub food.

Approaching Denny Wood

Blackwell Common and the Dark Water

Outline

Dark Water car-park – King's Copse Inclosure – Dark Water – Blackwell Common – Gatewood Bridge – Dark Water car-park.

Summary

This $2\frac{1}{2}$ mile walk explores a remote corner of the Forest, almost in the shadow of the vast Fawley oil-refinery on Southampton Water. The Dark Water and its valley, the focus of this circuit, were a favourite haunt of WH Hudson, the novelist and naturalist. In the spring months, the flora of the area is particularly outstanding. A notable specimen is the common dog violet, that can grow up to 8 inches in height.

Attractions

The Dark Water runs for just a few miles from its source, a mile or two above King's Copse Inclosure, down to the Solent at nearby Lepe. The river is crossed twice on this circuit. In the heart of the inclosure, the wooden footbridge provides the perfect location for a game of Pooh sticks. The more sedate visitor, on the other hand, may care to look out for the numerous waterboatmen that inhabit the river at this point. *Notonecta glauca* is a carnivorous bug, armed with a piercing, sucking beak. Be warned – this can inflict a sharp bite on an intruding finger! The waterboatman is a most athletic creature, able not only to swim and dive but also to fly. Towards the end of the walk, the Dark Water is crossed once again at Gatewood Bridge, on the corner of Blackwood Common. At this point, the water is shallow and easily accessible, the perfect spot for cooling hot feet at the end of the walk.

Alongside the woodland paths within King's Copse Inclosure lie decaying tree trunks and branches. Decaying timber is home to that motley collection of creatures described as 'decomposers' in the food chain. All of nature's detritus – dead wood, fallen leaves, animal droppings and carcasses – provide the soil with nutrients that foster plant growth. The decomposers help in the breakdown of this natural rubbish. Lift up an old piece of tree trunk or peel off a decaying piece of bark; the decomposers will be disturbed from their vital task. It is fairly easy to spot half a dozen such creatures, with slugs, grubs, worms, red ants, centipedes and woodlice being hard at work in the inclosure.

Whilst youngsters are pretty adept at recognising wild flowers, insects, birds and animals, tree spotting is an altogether different proposition. With the exception of the oak, most other tree names are a complete mystery to many children. King's Copse Inclosure, a fine area of mixed woodland, provides an excellent location for identifying many of Britain's more common trees. To add an element of interest, see how many of the letters of the alphabet can be matched-up with a particular tree. Ash matches the letter 'A', beech 'B' and so on. A total of 10 should be within the grasp of most visitors, persuade David Attenborough to accompany you and 15 is a

Continued on page 60

Route 13

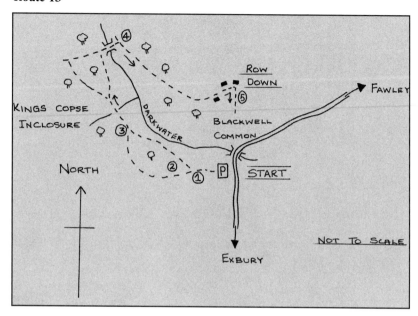

58

Route 13

Blackwell Common and the Dark Water   2.5 miles

Start

The Dark Water car-park lies on an unclassified road midway between Exbury and Blackfield, in the south-western corner of the New Forest. GR 433014.

1. *Walk to the western end of the Dark Water parking area, and continue directly ahead following a well-defined path that borders a fence on the left-hand side. In 300 yards, the path passes through a gateway before forking.*

2. *Bear to the right, and continue along the main path ahead. It drops down a slight slope before bearing to the left. In a few hundred yards, turn right at a T-junction.*

3. *Continue along a wide, potentially muddy ride. It descends to cross a tributary stream of the Dark Water. Fork to the right just beyond this tribulet, continue along the wide forest path ahead to a T-junction, and turn right down to a footbridge across the Dark Water.*

4. *Shortly after crossing the footbridge, turn right at a T-junction. In almost $\frac{1}{2}$ mile the path reaches a gateway where it leaves King's Copse Inclosure to emerge onto Blackwell Common. Continue ahead along the gravelled track until you reach King's Copse House on the left-hand side.*

5. *Bear sharp right alongside King's Copse House to follow a grassy path across Blackwell Common to reach the Fawley to Exbury road. Turn right at the road, cross the Dark Water at Gatewood Bridge, and a few yards up the hill is the parking area.*

Public Transport

Southampton to Langley buses pass through Blackfield, just 1 mile from the start of the walk. The service is operated by Solent Blue Line.

realistic target. Either way, a visit to King's Copse Inclosure should see you racing towards the Honourable Rank of Forester if you own a copy of the I-Spy Trees book!

Refreshments
There are no refreshment facilities on this route. A fine alternative is to pack a picnic which can be enjoyed alongside the Dark Water at journey's end.

Route finding in Kings Copse Inclosure

Route 14   4.5 miles

Beaulieu and Bucklers Hard

Outline
Beaulieu – Jarvis's Copse – Keeping Copse – Keeping Marsh – Bucklers
Hard – Beaulieu.

Summary
Two of the most popular tourist attractions in the Forest, a couple of miles apart on
the Beaulieu River. At Beaulieu, visitors explore the Palace House, the Abbey ruins
and the National Motor Museum, whilst at Bucklers Hard we find a traditional
shipbuilding village whose wide main street runs down to the banks of the river.
This $4\frac{1}{2}$ mile circuit explores the Beaulieu River between these two villages, a
peaceful nature trail that will provide a welcome antidote to the crowds that flock to
Lord Beaulieu's Estate.

Attractions
Beaulieu stands at the tidal limit of the Beaulieu River, 5 miles from the Solent. The
settlement's original name of Bellus Locus – literally 'beautiful place' – describes
this sheltered and wooded spot in a nutshell. The 13th century saw the arrival of
Cistercian monks in the area, and the Latin name being changed to its Norman
French equivalent, Beau Lieu. With the dissolution of the monasteries under Henry
VIII, the ecclesiastical stones were removed to the Solent to help in the construction
of the coastal defences.

Beaulieu's Palace House has been the ancestral home of the Montagu Family
since 1538. Despite its splendour, this fine building was originally nothing more
than the gatehouse to Beaulieu Abbey! The Palace House is open to the public, and
contains an extensive collection of paintings and furniture. Equally, the ruinous
remains of the Abbey form the centrepiece of a monastic life exhibition. To
youngsters, however, these historical trifles will be incidental to the main attraction
at Beaulieu – the National Motor Museum. This quite superb exhibition contains
over 250 historic vehicles dating from 1895 to the present, including Donald
Campbell's 'Bluebird'.

The New Forest oaks formed the backbone of the British Navy for many
centuries. The tidal inlets and rivers that led off the Solent were at one time the
centre of the British shipbuilding industry. This is nowhere more true than at
Bucklers Hard, a village on the Beaulieu River that contributed three men-o'-war to
Nelson's fleet at Trafalgar. Between 1745 and 1822, a staggering 71 ships were built
here from the Forest oaks. The unusually wide street that runs through the village
down to the water's edge was designed to be wide enough to roll the local tree trunks
down to the 'hard' (or slipway). Today's village is a living museum. In addition to
the actual Maritime Museum, the homes of a labourer, shipwright and master
shipbuilder can be visited, as well as the New Inn of 1793. Incidentally, by walking

Continued on page 64

61

Route 14

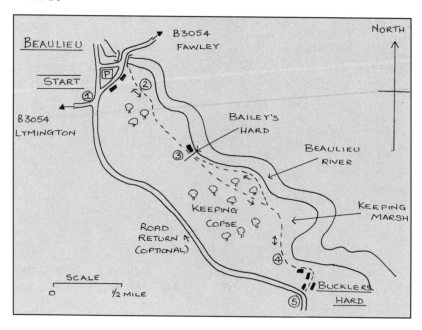

Route 14

Beaulieu and Bucklers Hard   4.5 miles

Start

Beaulieu lies on the B3054, 6 miles north-east of Lymington. As you enter the village from the west, there is a signposted car-park on the right-hand side. GR 386022.

1. *Return to the B3054 (Beaulieu millpond opposite) and turn right. In a short distance, just past the Montagu Arms, turn right onto a private road. Follow this unmetalled access road past the local fire station and onto a gate/stile.*

2. *Cross the stile and follow the sandy track ahead for 250 yards across open fields to a cattle grid. Beyond the cattle grid, the path passes around a small creek and cuts through a corner of Jarvis's Copse before reaching a large open field. Follow the left-hand edge of this field to a stile and a cottage in the far corner.*

3. *The waymarked footpath proceeds beyond the cottage, through to Bucklers Hard, passing through Keeping Copse en route. Eventually the path emerges from the trees to border Keeping Marsh, before passing behind a boatyard.*

4. *Turn left at the entrance to the boatyard to follow the waymarked 'Riverside Path' into the heart of Bucklers Hard.*

5. *To return either pass up through Bucklers Hard main street, turn right at the road junction and follow the unclassified road back to Beaulieu (busy in season) or retrace your steps. When retracing your steps, there is an excellent diversion. Just as you enter Keeping Copse, the path forks. Bear right onto the 'Riverside Path'. This follows the west bank of the Beaulieu River for almost 1 mile before rejoining the main right-of-way just before Bailey's Hard.*
   NB. *The circular walk involves returning along a somewhat uninteresting road from Bucklers Hard. I thoroughly recommend that you retrace your steps back to Beaulieu and take in the quite exceptional 'Riverside Path'.*

Public Transport

Lymington to Hythe buses, operated by Wiltshire and Dorset Buses, pass through Beaulieu.

to Bucklers Hard you will avoid its astronomical parking fees – cars are charged per passenger rather than per vehicle!

Between Beaulieu and Bucklers Hard, the walk explores a fascinating mixture of woodland, fieldpaths, river-bank and mudflats. Alongside Jarvis's Copse lies a small muddy inlet running off the Beaulieu River. The moisture-loving plants found here include rushes, reeds and willow herb. Further on, Keeping Copse is an extensive area of mixed woodland. The large number of oaks, however, stand as testimony to the area's shipbuilding history. The final approach to Bucklers Hard sees the path pass Keeping Marsh. These mudflats provide yet another fascinating habitat, where plants such as glasswort and orache thrive.

Refreshments
In Bucklers Hard, the Yachtsman's Bar and the Master Builder's Hotel provide ample refreshment. Back in Beaulieu, search out the Old Bakehouse Tea Room in the High Street.

Bucklers Hard

64

Hatchet Pond

Outline
A circumnavigation of Hatchet Pond.

Summary
Hatchet Pond, lying at the eastern end of Beaulieu Heath, is widely recognised as the most beautiful pond on the Forest. This 2 mile circuit explores the extensive perimeter of the pond, as well as its feeder streams. The terrain is generally level, although the frequent boggy patches make waterproof footwear an absolute necessity.

Attractions
Although Hatchet Pond might appear to be shaped like a short-handled axe, its name is actually derived from a former hatch gate that gave access to the open heath from enclosed farmland. The pond was originally the site of a number of marl pits, which were flooded to supply water for a mill in nearby East Boldre.

The pond provides a natural focus for a rich variety of wildfowl. Even the most lethargic birdwatcher would very quickly spot species such as coot, moorhen, gulls, swans, mallard and muscovy duck. The coot and moorhen are both part of the *Rallidae* family, and to the uninformed are often confused. The moorhen, however, is recognisable by its red beak and white tail feathers. The coot is much less colourful, with only a white bill standing out from its uniform blackness. The muscovy duck is a most unattractive creature – bird books are rather more polite and simply describe the bird as being quite distinctive! The crest, the bare red wattle and the knob on the bill make the muscovy duck easy to spot, together with its most clumsy form. *Cairina moschata* finds flying so difficult that its nest is usually built on the ground.

The slightly elevated open ground at the west of the pond is Beaulieu Heath. An airfield was built on this site in 1942, and the site saw tremendous action in 1944 when major attacks were launched on flying bombs and invasion targets. The airfield was functional until 1959, when several of the runways were removed. The OS sheet labels the site as a 'model aircraft flying area'. At the end of the walk, it is worth driving back the mile-or-so along the Lymington road to reach the former airfield. Youngsters will certainly enjoy watching the model craft performing extraordinary feats in the skies. The airfield car-park is at GR 353000.

Refreshments
Other than the ice-cream van that visits the Hatchet Pond car-park regularly, there are no refreshment facilities on this route. Hungry visitors will have to continue into Beaulieu, a couple of miles away.

Route 15

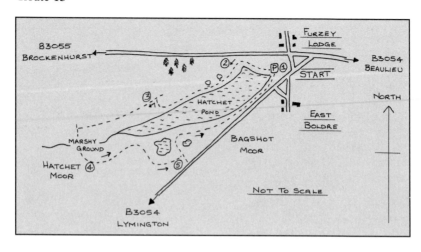

66

Route 15

Hatchet Pond   2 miles

Start

>   *Hatchet Pond car-park lies 2 miles west of Beaulieu on the B3054 Lymington road, at its junction with the B3055 Brockenhurst road. GR 369017.*

1. *Walk along the north-eastern shore of Hatchet Pond, on around the pond's northern tip and down the opposite bank to a row of pine trees that border the water's edge.*

2. *Continue alongside the shore of Hatchet Pond, staying with the footpath as it bends away from the pond to a T-junction.*

3. *Turn left and follow the chalk-flint path for 600 yards to a T-junction. It initially runs parallel to Hatchet Pond, before running a course slightly above the pond's feeder streams. At the T-junction, turn left and cross the marshy ground ahead through which the feeder streams flow. You were warned about waterproof footwear!*

4. *Continue uphill, bearing left at any junctions, as the path circumnavigates the damp ground at the western end of Hatchet Pond. When the path reaches the south-western corner of the pond, bear right, away from the water's edge, up to a second smaller pond. Follow the path around this pond until you join the Hatchet Moor car-park access road.*

5. *Turn left and head down the access road as far as a turning circle at its end, just before Hatchet Pond. Turn right, and follow a path which runs alongside the pond, back to the start of the walk. The final 200 yards of the walk are along a level gravelled path that is sandwiched between the pond and the adjoining B3054.*

Public Transport

Wiltshire and Dorset Buses run a service between Lymington, Beaulieu and Hythe which passes Hatchet Pond.

Keyhaven

Keyhaven and Pennington Marshes

Outline
Keyhaven – Keyhaven Marshes – Pennington Marshes – Pennington –
Solent Way – Keyhaven.

Summary
Keyhaven's small harbour lies on the North Solent shoreline, a quiet and unspoilt
corner of what is often a hectic stretch of water. To the north-east of Keyhaven lies a
vast area of wild marsh, mud flats and creeks. Level tracks, lanes, fieldpaths and a
section of the Solent Way are followed across this fascinating landscape, where the
vast numbers of sea-birds make field-glasses an absolute necessity! Although this
walk lies outside the New Forest's official boundaries, it gives a flavour of the
coastline in this corner of Hampshire.

Attractions
Keyhaven is located alongside a tidal inlet on the North Solent coast. The harbour
is a delightful backwater, providing safe moorings for dozens of small boats and
yachts. A seasonal ferry runs from the harbour to Hurst Castle, located just outside
the village at the end of a $1\frac{1}{2}$ mile long spit of pebbles. The alternative is a hard slog
along a pebble causeway! Hurst Castle was built by Henry VIII as part of his south
coast defences, although the fortification saw active service as recently as the last
war. The castle is open to the public, and makes a fascinating excursion at the end of
the walk.

Keyhaven and Pennington Marshes form the central focus of this walk. This
area of coastal marsh, shingle beach and lonely foreshore is a mecca for
ornithologists. On the landward side of the coast path lie a number of pools. Terns,
the grey phalarope, ruff and the little stint are but four of the delightful species
found in this particular habitat. The foreshore is rich in waders, with turnstones,
oystercatchers, lapwings, dunlins, redshanks and black-tailed godwits being just a
few names to conjure with. My own personal favourites are the dark-bellied brent
geese that gather along the coast in the winter months. As flocks of these birds
descend upon the lonely marshes, the scene brings to life those marvellously
atmospheric paintings of the late Sir Peter Scott.

A section of the Solent Way is followed back to Keyhaven from Pennington.
This path runs for 58 miles from Emsworth, just east of Portsmouth, to Milford-on-
Sea. It crosses shingle beaches, waymarked country lanes and parts of the New
Forest, as well as making use of four ferry crossings. These run from Hurst Castle to
Keyhaven, Hythe to Southampton, Hamble to Warsash, and Gosport to Ports-
mouth. The section of the Solent Way that borders the Keyhaven and Pennington
Marshes enjoys far-reaching views to the Isle of Wight. The regular ferries that ply
between Lymington and Yarmouth on the Isle of Wight are certain to catch your

Continued on page 72

69

Route 16

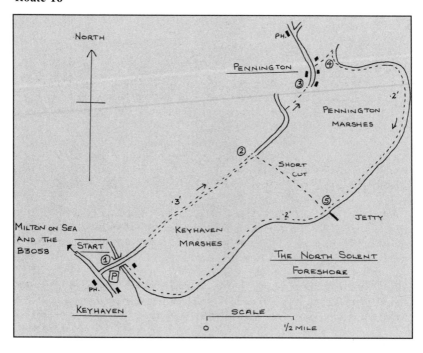

Keyhaven Marshes

Route 16

Keyhaven and Pennington Marshes   3 or 5 miles

Start

Keyhaven lies 2 miles east of Milford-on-Sea, on an unclassified road that connects with the B3058. As you enter the village, turn left at the Gun Inn and follow a cul-de-sac lane for just 200 yards to a parking area overlooking Keyhaven's harbour. GR 306295. (If this parking area is full, use the public car-park in Keyhaven and walk back to this spot.)

1. *Continue along the lane as it crosses the harbour bridge. In just 200 yards, the tarmac road ends and becomes a gravelled track. Follow this track for 1 mile alongside the northern boundary of Keyhaven Marshes, until it joins a quiet lane.*

2. *Follow the lane ahead for $\frac{1}{4}$ mile until, just past a left-hand bend, a footpath heads off on the right-hand side. Follow this footpath for 400 yards until it joins a lane. (For the shorter walk, turn right at point 2 and head directly across the marshes to the coast. Rejoin the walk at point 5.)*

3. *Follow this lane past Oxey Farm House, a row of cottages and Oxey Barn. 100 yards past Oxey Barn, cross a stile on the right just before reaching a house. (If you continue along this road for just 200 yards, you will reach the Chequers Inn.)*

4. *Beyond the stile, the path follows the right-hand bank of a small creek until it reaches a sluice gate. Continue on the path to the right of the sluice, following the Solent coast for just over 1 mile to a small jetty. The shorter walk rejoins us at this point.*

5. *Continue along the coast path, following the low sea-walls for $1\frac{1}{2}$ miles back into Keyhaven.*

Public Transport

Wiltshire and Dorset Buses run a service between Bournemouth and Lymington that passes through Milford-on-Sea, just 1 mile from the start of the walk in Keyhaven.

eye on this walk, along with the many other commercial and pleasure craft that pass through the Solent's waters each day.

Refreshments
At the end of the walk, the Gun in Keyhaven offers a good range of bar food. Just off the actual route in Pennington lies the Chequers (see map). This pub welcomes children in the eating area and, being near the walk's halfway point, is worth seeking out.

Keyhaven Harbour

Useful Information

ROUTES IN ORDER OF DIFFICULTY

As an experienced walker, I would class all of the walks in this book as very easy if I were tackling them on my own. However, these are Family Walks and the grading should be read with this in mind. They apply to a fairly active seven or eight year old, rather than a hardened veteran of the hills!

Very Easy Walks:

Route   3 – *Fritham and Eyeworth Pond.*
Route   9 – *Wilverley Inclosure and the Naked Man.*
Route 10 – *Ober Water.*
Route 15 – *Hatchet Pond.*

Easy Walks:

Route   1 – *Godshill Inclosure and Castle Hill.*
Route   5 – *The Rufus Stone.*
Route   6 – *The Knightwood Oak and Holidays Hill Inclosure.*
Route 13 – *Blackwell Common and the Dark Water.*

Moderately Difficult:

Route   2 – *Hampton Ridge and Latchmore Bottom.*
Route   4 – *Linford Inclosure.*
Route   7 – *Dur Hill Down and Whitten Pond.*
Route   8 – *Burley and Turf Hill.*
Route 11 – *Lyndhurst and Longwater Lawn.*
Route 12 – *Beaulieu Road and Denny Wood.*
Route 14 – *Beaulieu and Bucklers Hard.*
Route 16 – *Keyhaven and Pennington Marshes.*

BUS OPERATORS IN THE AREA

Wiltshire and Dorset – Telephone Lymington 672382
Poole 673555

Solent Blue Line – Telephone Southampton 226235
Eastleigh 618233

Maybury Coaches – Telephone Cranborne 444

TOURIST INFORMATION CENTRES IN THE AREA

The New Forest Tourist Information Centre,
High Street,
Lyndhurst,
Hampshire SO43 7NV. Telephone: (0703) 282269.

The office to contact for information on the New Forest – buses, camp sites, leisure facilities, local events, etc. Open all year.

Seasonal Tourist Information Centres:

Lymington – Telephone (0590) 672422.
Ringwood – Telephone (0425) 470896.
Fordingbridge – Telephone (0425) 545600.

Auction ring at New Forest Pony Sales – route 12.

WET WEATHER ALTERNATIVES

Completely or partly under cover.

Museums

Beaulieu – National Motor Museum. See under 'Historic Buildings'.

Breamore – Carriage and Countryside Museums. See under 'Historic Buildings'.

Bucklers Hard – Maritime Museum. Displays relating to the village's shipbuilding heritage. Open daily from 10 am.

Fordingbridge – Shering Museum. Everyday objects of the not-so-remote past. Check opening times with the local Tourist Information Centre.

New Forest Museum & Visitor Centre, Lyndhurst. Open daily throughout the year from 10 am.

New Milton – Sammy Miller Museum. One of the world's largest collections of motorcycles. Open daily 10–4.30.

Paulton's Romany and Village Life Museums. See under 'Other places of interest'.

HISTORIC BUILDINGS

Beaulieu – Palace House, Abbey Ruins and Motor Museum. Open daily from 10 am.

Breamore House – Elizabethan manor, Carriage and Countryside Museums. Open April to September. Check at local Tourist Information Centre for days and hours.

Calshot Castle. Part of Henry VIII's coastal defence chain. Open April to September 10–6.

Hurst Castle. Part of Henry VIII's coastal defence chain. Open April to September 10–6 and winter weekends.

Rockbourne Roman Villa. Over 50 rooms, that include mosaic floors and bath house. Museum displays. Open April to September.

OTHER PLACES OF INTEREST

Calshot Crafts Centre. Open daily 10–5.

Eling Tide Mill. Britain's only tide mill in regular production of wholemeal flour. Telephone (0703) 869575 for times.

Longdown Dairy Farm. Working dairy farm. Open daily Easter to October 11–5.

Lymington Vineyard. Open May to September, excluding Saturdays.

New Forest Brass Rubbing Centre, St Mark's Church, Pennington. Open school holiday weekdays 10–12.

New Forest Butterfly Farm, Ashurst. Open daily Easter to October 10–5.

New Forest Cider, Burley. Open most times throughout the year.

New Forest Owl Sanctuary, Ringwood. Open daily 10–dusk.

Paulton's Park – pleasure park that includes Romany and Village Life Museums. Open daily during the season 10–6.30.

* It is important to check opening times with either the attraction itself or the nearest Tourist Information Centre since days and times are subject to change. The Tourist Information Centres can also advise on attractions such as swimming pools and leisure centres.

1:25 000 SHEETS USED IN PREPARING THE WALKS

Just one map was used in the preparation of this book: Ordnance Survey Outdoor Leisure 22 New Forest.

No self-respecting visitor to the Forest should be without this sheet!

Holidays Hill Inclosure – route 6.

THE FAMILY WALKS SERIES

The publishers welcome suggestions for further titles in this series; and will be pleased to consider manuscripts relating to Derbyshire from new or established authors.

Scarthin Books of Cromford, in the Peak District, are also leading second-hand and antiquarian book-sellers, and are eager to purchase specialised material, both ancient and modern.

Contact Dr D. J. Mitchell, 0624-823272.